The Not-So-Friendly Friend

How to Set Boundaries for Healthy Friendships

Christina Furnival
Illustrated by Katie Dwyer

The Not-So-Friendly Friend
Copyright © 2021 Christina Furnival

Published by:
PESI Publishing & Media
PESI, Inc.
3839 White Ave.
Eau Claire, WI 54703

Illustrations: Katie Dwyer
Cover: Katie Dwyer
Layout: Katie Dwyer, Jennifer Wilson-Gaetz, Amy Rubenzer
ISBN: 9781683734635

PESI Publishing
pesipublishing.com

Dedication

To my children, Isla and Sterling, and to any child
who reads this book: You are precious, and you
deserve to be treated as such—especially by anyone
lucky enough to call themselves your friend.

To my parents, Jim and Lisa, who have always
been there for me. Thank you for everything.

And to my husband, Tom, who makes me feel like gold
every single day. Thank you for encouraging my book-
writing dream and for giving me the freedom to leap.

There once was a girl
who was new at her school.

To make some good friends she used the Golden Rule.

She treated her classmates
how she liked
to be treated.

She was helpful and loving,
and her hugs were the sweetest.

It was easy to like her.
She was lovely and kind,

a good problem solver
who had a bright mind.

She shared
and took turns,
was as fair
as they come.

She used words
(not her body)
to solve
any problem.

But try as she might,
not everyone liked her.

There was one other kid
who found reason to fight her.

At first she tried harder
to be this kid's friend.

But this kid was not nice
and teased her to no end.

Unkind words and rude actions
would make her heart frown.
When they played together,
she was left feeling down.

She realized this friend
was no friend at all,
'cause someone who loves you
won't make you feel small.

Staying true
to herself
and her
beautiful
heart,

she created some boundaries—
the right place to start.

If this kid was nice,
she'd play and have fun.

But if they were not,
then she'd say...

"I'll play with true friends
who make me feel good
and treat me with love,
just as a friend should."

"When you're ready to change
and be nice again,

you're welcome to join
and play with us then."

The lesson she learned
she still uses today.
She won't put up with bullies,
it's never okay.

She stands up for herself
and how she wants to be treated,
and does so respectfully.
She doesn't get heated.

And if she needs help
or doesn't know what to say,
she asks a trusted adult
to show her the way.

With boundaries in place,
healthy friendships can grow.

You'll have fun and feel safe, with your heart all aglow.

Note to Parents and Professionals

The Not-So-Friendly Friend, the first story in the *Capable Kiddos* series, involves the topic of friendship and boundaries.

When it comes to boundaries, we might not typically think about teaching young children how to set them. However, research shows that setting firm limits in peer relationships can be helpful in decreasing bullying.

Additionally, boundary setting is linked with greater self-care, self-worth, self-respect, and assertiveness. By teaching this skill to children, we open them up to a future of healthy relationships.

Conversation Starters and Discussion Questions

What is a boundary?

A boundary is a limit. It can be physical, like a fence or a barrier. Or it can be an expectation set between people as protection. This book talks about boundaries that we set with other people, including what we find acceptable (or not) in their actions toward others or us. Setting a boundary shows that you love and care for yourself and how others treat you.

When and why might we want to set a boundary?

Pay attention to and notice how you are feeling, which is also known as being self-aware. If you feel uncomfortable or upset, your emotions are trying to tell you something. It might be a sign that you want to set a boundary. This could be because someone is in your physical space; is not valuing your thoughts, opinions, or beliefs; is not respecting your feelings; or is trying to control you.

Is setting a boundary easy or hard?

Setting boundaries is often not easy, especially when you are new to it. You might be afraid it will make the other person mad, but a true friend will support you in doing what is best for you. If they do get mad, then you have learned that they aren't a very good friend. Just like a muscle grows stronger with more exercise, boundary-setting skills grow stronger with more practice. It will get easier and you will get better at it!

What is a good friend? What do they say or do?

Good friends are kind, helpful, considerate, dependable, honest, and communicative. They do things to make you feel good, happy, supported, and loved. Friends are fun to be with, like to share with you, consider your feelings, and use kind words to solve conflicts with you. They want you to be your true self, and you want that for them too!

Have you (or your grown-up) ever had a friend who treated you in a way you didn't like? How could you set a boundary with them? Let's practice.

You can say what feels right to you! Here's an example: "You are not treating me like a good friend, and I am not okay with that, so I will not play with you right now. You can play with me again when you're ready to be nice." This will kindly get your respectful, assertive message across.

If I set a boundary, am I being mean?

Boundary setting may make you feel like you're being mean, but really you're not! When a person sets a boundary, they are actually being nice to the person we should all be nicest too: ourselves. Showing ourselves love and respect is one of the best things we can do throughout life.

About the Author

Christina Furnival, MS, LPCC, is a wife, mother of two, writer, author, and licensed mental health therapist. With over a decade of experience in the field, she is passionate about helping parents and children grow their skill sets, overcome challenges, and gain confidence to live happy, fulfilling lives.

Her meaningful stories in the *Capable Kiddos* series serve as entertaining and enlightening resources to empower children and to make them feel capable of managing tough situations and their accompanying emotions. Visit her at ChristinaFurnival.com and on Instagram at @CapableKiddosBooks.

About the Illustrator

Katie Dwyer, is a freelance illustrator from sunny California. Her playful children's illustrations have been featured in Pottery Barn Kids, and her hand-lettering has been used for cards, signs, and murals in Pottery Barn as well as local markets. Her most recent book *When Daddy Goes Away* is available now.

When she isn't drawing, Katie can be found playing with her three little boys, watching movies, and eating good food with her husband. She has a passion for spreading joy and sharing art with children through her magical illustrations. Visit Katie at www.katiedwyerillustrations.com and on Instagram @katiedwyer.illustrations.